Cookies Recipes

Edition 1

By

Cheryl Green

Pretty Pink French Macarons

Ingredients:

for the macarons

1 cup almond flour

2 cups icing sugar

3 eggwhites

1/4 cup white sugar (granulated)

1/4 tsp cream of tartar

1/8 tsp salt (or a pinch)

drops of gel food colour (optional)

for the filling

3 tbsp fresh raspberry juice (pure)

1/4 cup salted butter

3/4 cup icing sugar

Cooking procedure for the macarons:

1. In a mixing bowl, sift the almond flour and the icing sugar. Mix thoroughly. Set aside.

2. In a separate mixing bowl, beat the egg whites, salt, cream of tartar, granulated sugar and drops of gel food colouring (using an electric mixer) until it forms a peak.

3. Combine the two (2) mixtures, the mixture #1 and the

mixture #2. Just use an eggbeater or spatula in mixing. Mix

Gently until smooth. Do not under-mix. Do not over-mix.

4. Place the mixture in an icing bag or pastry bag.

5. Pipe out 1 inch rounds on the baking tray with a baking

paper. (Bang the tray 3 times with the macarons on it, to release

the air inside the macarons.)

6. Let them sit out for 20-30 mins, or up to an hour.

7. Preheat the oven to 100 degrees celsius.

8. Bake the macarons for 18-20 minutes. (Just keep an eye, all

ovens bake differently.)

9. Remove the tray from the oven. Let it cool down before

removing the macarons from the tray.

For the filling:

1. In a mixing bowl, mix the softened butter, icing sugar and the raspberry juice. Then set aside.

   - Get a pair of macarons, put the filling in between. And you're done!

Note:

You can choose any filling as desired. Just omit the gel food colouring.

Enjoy and share it with family!

Oatmeal Cookies

Ingredients:

1 1/2 cup quick-cooking oats

1/2 cup butter, softened

3/4 cup all-purpose flour

1/2 cup white sugar

1/2 cup brown sugar

1/2 teaspoon vanilla extract

1/2 teaspoon baking soda

1/2 teaspoon ground cinnamon

1/4 teaspoon baking powder

1/2 teaspoon salt

1 egg

Preparation:

1. In a mixing bowl, combine the butter and sugars.

2. In a separate small bowl, beat the egg and vanilla.

3. Combine the two (2) mixtures.

4. Add the flour, baking soda, cinnamon, baking powder, and salt. Mix evenly. Gradually add the oats and mix thoroughly.

5. Get the oven tray and put a wax/baking paper on it.

6. Using an ice cream scoop: scoop and drop the mixture on the wax/baking paper.

7. Preheat the oven to 150 degrees celsius.

8. Place inside the oven and bake for 20-25 minutes.

9. Remove from the oven and let it cool down, then serve.

Chocolate Crinkles

Ingredients:

2 cups all-purpose flour (sifted)

1 1/4 cup granulated sugar

1/2 cup unsalted butter (softened)

1/2 cup semi-sweet chocolate chips (melted)

2/3 cups unsweetened cocoa powder

1 teaspoon baking powder

4 pieces raw eggs

1 cup icing sugar

1 tbsp vanilla extract

1/2 teaspoon salt

Preparation:

1. In a mixing bowl, mix the softened butter and granulated sugar until smooth.

2. Add the cocoa powder and melted chocolate then mix again until evenly combined.

3. Add the eggs and vanilla extract and continue to mix until smooth.

4. Add the flour, salt, and baking powder. Mix again until all the ingredients are evenly distributed.

5. Refrigerate for at least 3-4 hours. Cover the mixing bowl with

a cling wrap.

6. Get the mixture from the refrigerator, then remove the cover.

7. Scoop the mixture using 1 tablespoon measuring spoon.

8. Roll the mixture using your palms until the shape becomes round.

9. Roll the chocolate balls over the icing sugar until fully covered.

10. Put the chocolate balls with icing sugar on the oven tray with baking paper. Each ball should be at least 2 inches apart.

11. Preheat oven to 120°C. Bake the chocolate balls for 15-20 minutes.

12. Remove from the oven and allow to cool down, then serve.

Oatmeal Chocolate Chip Cookies

Ingredients

1 1/2 cups packed brown sugar

1 cup butter or margarine, softened

1 teaspoon vanilla

1 egg

2 cups quick-cooking oats

1 1/2 cups Gold Medal all-purpose or unbleached flour

1 teaspoon baking soda

1/4 teaspoon salt

1 cup semisweet chocolate chips (6 oz)

1 cup chopped nuts, if desired

Preparation:

1. Heat oven to 350°F. In large bowl, stir brown sugar and butter until blended. Stir in vanilla and egg until light and fluffy. Stir in oats, flour, baking soda and salt; stir in chocolate chips and nuts.

2. Onto ungreased cookie sheet, drop dough by rounded tablespoonfuls about 2 inches apart.

3. Bake 10 to 12 minutes or until golden brown. Cool slightly; remove from cookie sheet to wire rack.

Broas (Ladyfinger Cookies)

Ingredients:

3 eggs, separated

80g (6 tablespoons) caster sugar

65g (8 tablespoons) sifted plain flour

2-3 tablespoons icing sugar for dusting

Preparation:

Preheat the oven to 170*C

Line two baking trays with parchment/baking paper.

In a large bowl, whisk the egg yolks with 1 tablespoon of the caster sugar until pale. Set aside.

In the bowl of your stand mixer, whip the egg whites until frothy/foamy.

Add the caster sugar, one tablespoon at a time and continue whipping until you get stiff peaks and the meringue is glossy.

Fold in the beaten egg yolks.

Add the sifted flour and gently fold until incorporated.

Spoon the mixture into a piping bag and pipe into 3.5 inch long strips.

Using a fine sieve, dust the cookies with icing sugar.

Bake in the preheated oven for 12 minutes.

Turn off the heat and with oven door slightly open, leave the trays in

the oven for 15 minutes more, to let the cookies dry.

Pinipig Cookies

Recipe 1:

Ingredients:

3 cups cassava flour

3 cups fried pinipig

1 tsp baking powder

1 tsp vanilla (optional)

1 cup margarine

1 cup sugar

3 pcs eggs

Instructions:

Sift cassava flour and baking powder. Mix with pinipig. Cream margarine and sugar. Add eggs one at a time.

Continue creaming until all eggs have been added.

Add flour mixture and mix well. Add vanilla. Drop by teaspoon on greased cookie sheets.

Bake until brown at 177oC (350oF).

Recipe 2

Makes about 2 dozen cookies

Ingredients:

3/4 cup (2 oz) pinipig (young sweet rice flakes)

1/2 cup (2.3 oz) all-purpose flour

1/2 tsp baking powder

1/8 tsp salt

1/4 cup unsalted butter, at room temperature

1/3 cup granulated sugar

1 large egg

1/4 tsp lemon zest

Directions:

Toast the pinipig. Heat a dry skillet over medium heat. Add the pinipig and toast while stirring often for about 5 minutes, until lightly browned and fragrant. Spread out the pinipig over a plate and allow to cool completely.

Preheat the oven to 350ºF / 175ºC with racks on the upper third and lower third of the oven. Prepare 2 parchment-lined or lightly greased half-sheet pans or cookie sheets.

Mix the dry ingredients. Place the flour, baking powder, and salt in a container with a tight lid. Cover and shake until thoroughly mixed.

Mix (Creaming Method). Beat the butter with the sugar until light and fluffy. Add the egg and continue beating to incorporation. Beat in the lemon zest.

Slowly add the dry ingredients to the butter mixture and continue mixing just until smooth and thoroughly incorporated. Gently fold in the cooled pinipig.

Drop. The cookie dough will be very sticky, so use two teaspoons or a small disher. Drop 12 evenly spaced portions for each sheet pan or cookie sheet. Each cookie dough portion is roughly equivalent to 1 heaping teaspoon, about the size of a cherry.

Bake the cookies at 350°F / 175°C for 10 to 12 minutes, or until lightly browned around the edges. Let the baked cookies rest on the sheets for a few minutes and transfer to a wire rack to cool completely.

Gooey Butter Cookies

Ingredients:

8 ounces cream cheese, softened

1/2 cup butter, softened

1 egg

1/2 teaspoon vanilla

1 (18 1/2 ounce) box white cake mix or yellow cake mix

confectioners sugar

Preparation:

Cream together cream cheese and butter. Add egg and vanilla, and cake mix and mix well. Refrigerate for at least 1 hour or until cookie dough is firm. Roll in 1 inch balls, then roll in confectioner's sugar.

Preheat oven to 350 degrees F. Bake cookies on an ungreased cookie sheet for 10-15 minutes or until cookies are slightly firm to touch.

Wait a minute or two before removing cookies to cooling racks. Dust with confectioners sugar.

Rosquillos

Recipe 1

This recipe yields 2-3 dozen small rings.

INGREDIENTS:

1 cup white wine

1 cup sugar

1 cup vegetable oil

1 cup vegetable shortening

3 tsp baking powder

2 tbsp anise extract

6 cups flour

granulated sugar for topping

PREPARATION

Pre-heat oven to 325 degrees.

Using a hand mixer, combine sugar, vegetable oil, vegetable shortening and baking powder together in a large mixing bowl. Add white wine and anise extract and mix well. Add flour a cup at a time. Mixture will seem dry or crumbly. You may want to use your hand to mix together the dough as you add the last 2 cups of flour.

Take out a small amount of dough and roll into a rope about 1/3" thick on an un-floured cutting board.

Cut into pieces about 4 inches long and join the two ends to form a doughnut shape or ring.

Carefully place on an ungreased cookie sheet and bake 15-18 minutes or until they become a golden color. Be careful not to burn the bottoms!

Let cool about 10 minutes, so the cookies do not fall apart as you lift them off with a spatula. While still warm, place in sugar to coat the tops.

Recipe 2

Ingredients:

6 cups flour

1 cup sugar

3 tsp baking powder

1 cup white wine

1 cup vegetable oil

1 cup vegetable shortening

2 tbsp anise extract

Procedure:

In a mixing bowl combine sugar, vegetable shortening, vegetable oil and baking powder.

When mixed, add anise extract and stir.

While stirring continuously add flour until dry or crumbly.

Use hands to mix together dough. Divide the dough into small pieces and flatten it on a floured table.

Use a flower shaped cookie cutter and cut the portions.

Lay the cut dough on a baking tray and set aside.

Pre-heat oven to 325 degrees Fahrenheit and bake cookies for 15 to 18 minutes.

Once cooked set aside and let it cool to prevent it from breaking down when removed from the tray.

Uraro cookies

Ingredients:

8 ounces butter

8 ounces rice flour

8 ounces superfine sugar

6 ounces arrowroot

6 eggs

Preparation:

Beat the butter to a cream.

Whisk the eggs to a strong froth.

Add them to the butter, stir in the flour a little at a time and beat the mixture well.

Break down all the lumps from the arrowroot and add it with the sugar to the other ingredients.

Mix all well together, drop the dough on a buttered tin (about 1″ in diameter and height) in pieces.

Bake the biscuits about 15 minutes in a slow oven.

Time: 15 minutes.

Sufficient to make from 3 to 4 dozen biscuits.

Red Velvet Cookies

INGREDIENTS

1 (8 ounce) brick cream cheese, room temperature

1/2 cup butter, room temperature (1 stick)

1 egg

1 tablespoon vanilla extract

1 (18 ounce) box red velvet cake mix

confectioners' sugar, for rolling and dusting

Preparation:

In a large bowl with an electric mixer, cream the cream cheese and butter until smooth.

Beat in the egg.

Beat in the vanilla extract.

Beat in the cake mix.

Cover and refrigerate for at least 2 hours to firm up so that you can roll the batter into balls. I've chilled batter overnight and it comes out fine.

After batter has chilled and you're ready to make the cookies, preheat the oven to 350°F.

Roll the chilled batter into tablespoon sized balls and then roll them in confectioner's sugar.

Place on an ungreased cookie sheet, 2 inches apart.

Bake 12 minutes. The cookies should remain soft and gooey.

Cool completely and sprinkle with more confectioners' sugar, if desired.

To make these devilishly rich, I also top the cookies with cream cheese frosting, which is simple to make. Or, if I'm making them for people I know have more of a savory tooth than sweet, I'll triple it to a full tablespoon.

Pineapple Brown Sugar Cookies

Ingredients:

1 cup butter, softened

1/2 cup firmly packed brown sugar

1 large egg

1 teaspoon vanilla

2 2/3 cups all-purpose flour

1 teaspoon baking powder

1/2 cup flaked coconut

1 (21 ounce) can pineapple filling, filling Solo brand

red food coloring or green food coloring

Preparation:

Cream together butter and brown sugar.

Beat in egg and vanilla.

Stir together flour and baking powder.

slowly add to creamed butter.

Chill 1/2 hour.

Roll one tablespoon of dough, make thumb print to fill with colored

pineapple.

Sprinkle with coconut.

Bake 400° for 8-10 minutes or until pale golden.

Lemon Cookies

Ingredients:

1 (18.25 ounce) package lemon cake mix

2 eggs

1/3 cup vegetable oil

1 teaspoon lemon extract

1/3 cup confectioners' sugar for

decoration

Preparation:

1. Preheat oven to 375 degrees F (190 degrees C).

2. Pour cake mix into a large bowl. Stir in eggs, oil, and lemon extract until well blended. Drop teaspoonfuls of dough into a bowl of confectioners' sugar. Roll them around until they're lightly covered. Once sugared, put them on an ungreased cookie sheet.

3. Bake for 6 to 9 minutes in the preheated oven. The bottoms will be light brown, and the insides chewy.

Caramel Apple Cookies

Ingredients:

½ cup vegetable shortening

1 ¼ cups packed light brown sugar

1 egg

½ cup apple juice, divided

2 ¼ cups all-purpose flour

1 teaspoon baking soda

¼ teaspoon salt

1 teaspoon ground cinnamon

¼ teaspoon ground cloves

1 cup apple, peeled and shredded

Frosting:

2 -3 tablespoons margarine, softened

⅓ cup packed light brown sugar

2 tablespoons water

1 ½ cups powdered sugar

2 -4 tablespoons milk

5 tablespoons finely crushed walnuts

Preparation:

Beat shortening and brown sugar in medium bowl until blended; beat in egg.

Mix in 1/4 cup apple juice.

Combined flour, baking soda, salt, and spices; mix in remaining 1/4 cup apple juice and apples.

Drop by teaspoonfuls, 2 inches apart, onto greased cookie sheets.

Bake at 350 until browned, 10 to 12 minutesCool on wire racks.

Spread with frosting and sprinkle each cookie with crushed walnuts.

Caramel Frosting: Heat margarine, brown sugar, and water over medium high heat in saucepan,stirring until sugar dissolves.

Remove from heat; beat in powdered sugar and enough milk to make spreadable consistency; use immediately.

If frosting begins to harden, return to low heat and stir in more milk.

Ham and Cheese Biscuits

Ingredients:

1 cup all purpose flour

1 teaspoon baking powder

1/4 teaspoon baking soda

1/4 cup butter, chilled and cut into small pieces

1/4 cup cheddar cheese, shredded

1/4 cup minced ham

1 teaspoon spicy brown mustard

2 tablespoons onion, minced

1/3 cup buttermilk

Container: cookie sheet, prepared with oil or no-stick cooking spray

Preparation:

Preheat oven to 450°.

In a medium sized bowl, sift together flour, baking powder and

baking soda.

Add butter and cut in with pastry blender until mixture looks like

coarse meal.

Blend in cheese, ham, mustard, and onions.

Add buttermilk, stirring until dough is soft.

Knead lightly on floured board. Roll to 1/2 inch thickness. Cut with a

2" cutter and place on prepared baking sheet. Bake 10 minutes or

until golden in color.

Chocolate Cookies

Ingredients:

- 1/4 cup (28g) of coconut flour sifted

1/4 cup (54g) of coconut oil or butter

1/3 cup (28g) of coco powder

3 eggs

sweetener of choice (same as 1/3 cup of sugar)

1/4 teaspoon of salt

1/4 teaspoon vanilla Essence

Preparation:

- Melt butter or oil stir in coco powder and leave to cool.

- In a bowl mix eggs with sugar or sweetener, vanilla essence and salt.

- Stir in coco mixture then add the sifted coconut flour to the batter until there are no lumps. - - Leave the batter for 5 minutes to rest and thicken up.

- Drop or pipe mixture on lined backing tray cook on 175'c for 10-15minutes

- makes about 16 cookies

Nutella Choco Chip Cookies with Almonds and Walnuts

Ingredients:

1 cup sweet unsalted butter, room temperature

1 cup nutella

1 cup granulated sugar

1 cup brown sugar or 1

cup light muscovado sugar, packed

2 large eggs

2 cups all-purpose flour

1 tsp baking soda

1 cup semi-sweet choco chips

1 cup white chocolate chips

1/2 cup chopped walnuts

1/2 cup chopped almonds

Preparation:

1. Preheat oven to 325 degrees F.

2. Have ready at least 2 baking sheets lined with parchment paper.

3. with an electric mixer, cream butter until smooth.

4. Add nutella and both sugars and beat until combined well.

5. Add egg and beat well.

6. Stir in flour and baking soda gradually until well combined.

7. Stir in chocolate chips by hand.

8. Using an ice cream scoop or a spoon, scoop out small portions of dough and drop onto parchment lined cookie sheets, leaving 2" gap between each cookie.

9. Bake for about 15 minutes or until cookies are just firm around the edges- don't overbake- if you wait until they are brown on top, they will be too hard.

10. Slide parchment sheet, cookies and all, carefully off pan and onto your counter, set a new piece of parchment paper onto your baking sheet and repeat until all dough is baked.

11. Meanwhile, as the next batch bakes, remove baked cookies from the parchment and let cool completely on wire racks.

12. Wipe off the crumbs from the old sheet of parchment and

you can reuse it for your next batch.

13. These will keep about 5-7 days stored in a cookie tin (for crisp cookies) or an airtight plastic container (for softer cookies).

Brownie Cookies

Ingredients:

7 tablespoons butter

10 tablespoons cocoa, divided

1 cup sugar

2 eggs

3/4 cup flour

1 teaspoon baking powder

1/4 teaspoon salt

3/4 cup chocolate chips

Preparation:

Melt butter in small saucepan on stove. Whisk in 6 tablespoons of cocoa (reserving the rest) until well combined and smooth. Remove from heat and let cool.

In small bowl combine flour, remaining 4 tablespoons cocoa, baking powder and salt. Stir just to blend. Set aside.

In mixing bowl, combine, cocoa/butter mixture, sugar and eggs.

Slowly add in flour mixture. Make sure to combine well.

Stir in chocolate chips.

Refrigerate dough for a minimum of 2 hours.

Preheat oven to 350 degrees. Drop dough by teaspoonfuls onto greased cookie sheets.

Bake for 8-10 minutes. Remove from oven and let sit for 10 minutes before removing to cooling racks.

See more at Melt butter in small saucepan on stove. Whisk in 6 tablespoons of cocoa (reserving the rest) until well combined and smooth. Remove from heat and let cool.

In small bowl combine flour, remaining 4 tablespoons cocoa, baking powder and salt. Stir just to blend. Set aside.

In mixing bowl, combine, cocoa/butter mixture, sugar and eggs.

Slowly add in flour mixture. Make sure to combine well.

Stir in chocolate chips.

Refrigerate dough for a minimum of 2 hours.

Preheat oven to 350 degrees. Drop dough by teaspoonfuls onto greased cookie sheets.

Bake for 8-10 minutes. Remove from oven and let sit for 10 minutes before removing to cooling racks.

Danish Butter Cookies

Ingredients:

125g butter

45g icing sugar

135g plain/all purpose flour

1tsp vanilla essence

1/2tsp baking powder

*I always like to use salted butter, simply because I like the hit of saltiness among the sweet, but by all means use unsalted if you prefer.

**The baking powder is optional. Most butter cookie recipes are without it, but I like to give my cookies a bit extra crisp fluffiness.

Preparation:

These have got to be the easiest cookies I've ever made. All done in one bowl, with a hand mixer. Simply cream together the butter and icing sugar until light and creamy. Add the sifted flour and baking powder and mix in. Add the vanilla essence and beat in. And the batter is done!

Line a cookie sheet with baking paper. Spoon everything into a piping bag fitted with a star tip and pipe into circles, or whatever shape you want. I found that the batter was a bit too stiff for piping, so I gave it a couple seconds in the microwave until it was pipable. Take care not to nuke it for more than 5-10 seconds at a time though, or you might end up with a melted butter soup. Bake at 150°C for 12-15 minutes until lightly browned.

Eggnog Cookies

Ingredients:

1/4 cup all purpose flour

2 egg whites

1/8 teaspoon baking powder

1/2 cup sugar

1/4 teaspoon vanilla extract

Preparation:

Preheat the oven to 275° F or 140° C.

Prepare cookie sheets with parchment paper and set aside.

Sift all purpose flour and baking powder and set aside.

Beat the egg whites in the bowl until they start to foam and stiff, add sugar little by little and beat until meringue is glossy with stiff peaks.

Fold in all purpose flour then add the vanilla extract.

Attach the coupling into a piping bag but don't put any icing nozzle.

Spoon the Icing mixture into the bag.

If you dont have a piping bag you can use wax paper shaped into a cone or a ziploc bag with the tip snipped.

Pipe the Icing batter like a flat coin sized rounds about 1 1/2" in diameter on the parchment-paper-lined cookie sheets.

Make sure to put space between cookies one inch apart.

Bake until lightly toasted, about 12 to 15 minutes.

Leave to cool in the baking pans

Egg Yolk Cookies

Ingredients:

Cake Flour 150g

Corn Flour 50g

Potato Flour 20g

Castor Sugar 60g

Cooked Yolk 2 (mashed)

Cold Butter 90g +/-

Egg wash ~ yolk + little of milk

Preparation:

Combine all flour, sifted.

Add sugar into flour mixture

Next, add Mashed cooked yolk

Cut cold butter into small cubes, pour all into flour mixture

Use fingertip to rub the butter into flour till crumbly or use hand

mixer slow beat to mix till crumbly (don't over beat)

Use hand to form a dough

Place dough between plastic sheet, I use 2 X 0.5cm thick sticks for leveling (even thickness).

Use your desired cookie cutter to cut out the shape.

Brushed with egg wash

Bake in preheated oven 350F / 180C for 15 minutes

The original recipe without potato flour, I have added some and taste more crunchy.

If it's too dry to form a dough, add a little butter.

Melting moments cookies

Ingredients:

125 g butter

1/3 cup icing sugar

1 t sp vanilla extract

3/4 cup of flour

1/4 cup of corn flour

Jam & cream for decoration

Preparation:

1. preheat the oven to 180 degrees

2. in a large bowl add butter , vanilla & sugar , beat until smooth & creamy

3. mix together flour & corn flour , add to the butter mixture , mix until form fluffy dough

4. take table spoon of mixture , roll into balls & place onto a tray. Using fork dipped icing sugar slightly squash each biscuit

5. baked for 12-16 minutes

6. remove biscuit from the oven , let it cool completely

7. spread with buttercream onto one half of the cooled biscuits , spread jam on the other half , then put the buttercream biscuit above the jam biscuit.

Peanut Cookies

Ingredients:

450g Peanuts

230g Peanut Oil

250g Caster Sugar

1/2tsp Salt

450g Plain Flour

Glazing:

2 Egg Yolks

Preparation:

Preheat oven to 165°C.

In a blender, grind the peanuts into a powder. Being careful not to over grind as it will turn into a soft paste.

Place all the ingredients into a blender. Blend until well combined.

Divide the dough into small round pieces.

Arrange in a baking tray and brush a layer of egg yolk on top of the cookies.

Bake in the oven for 20 to 25 minutes or until light golden brown.

Black and White Striped Cookies

Ingredients:

Vanilla dough

1 1/4 cups all-purpose flour (about 5 1/2 ounces)

1/8 teaspoon salt

1/2 cup powdered sugar

1/4 cup butter, softened

1 large egg yolk

1 1/2 teaspoons vanilla extract

2 tablespoons ice water

Chocolate dough:

3/4 cup all-purpose flour (about 3 1/3 ounces)

1/3 cup unsweetened cocoa

1/8 teaspoon salt

1 cup powdered sugar

1/4 cup butter, softened

1 large egg yolk

1/2 teaspoon vanilla extract

2 tablespoons ice water

Cooking instructions:

To prepare vanilla dough, lightly spoon 1 1/4 cups flour into dry

measuring cups; level with a knife. Combine 1 1/4 cups flour and 1/8 teaspoon salt, stirring well with a whisk. Place 1/2 cup sugar, 1/4 cup butter, and 1 egg yolk in a medium bowl; beat with a mixer at medium speed until smooth. Beat in 1 1/2 teaspoons vanilla. Gradually add flour mixture to butter mixture, beating at low speed just until combined. Sprinkle 2 tablespoons ice water over surface of dough; beat just until moist. (Dough will be slightly crumbly.) Press dough into a 4-inch circle on plastic wrap; cover and chill 1 hour or until firm.

To prepare chocolate dough, lightly spoon 3/4 cup flour into dry measuring cups; level with a knife. Combine 3/4 cup flour, cocoa, and 1/8 teaspoon salt, stirring well with a whisk. Place 1 cup sugar, 1/4 cup butter, and 1 egg yolk in a medium bowl; beat with a mixer at medium speed until smooth. Beat in 1/2 teaspoon vanilla. Gradually add cocoa mixture to butter mixture, beating at low speed just until combined. Sprinkle 2 tablespoons ice water over surface of dough; beat just until moist. Press dough into a 4-inch circle on plastic wrap; cover and chill 1 hour or until firm.

Slightly overlap 2 sheets of plastic wrap on a slightly damp surface. Unwrap and place chilled vanilla dough on plastic wrap. Cover dough with 2 additional sheets of overlapping plastic wrap. Roll dough, still covered, into a 12 x 8-inch rectangle. Place dough in freezer 5 minutes or until plastic wrap can easily be removed. Remove top sheets of plastic wrap.

Slightly overlap 2 sheets of plastic wrap on a slightly damp surface. Unwrap and place chilled chocolate dough on plastic wrap. Cover dough with 2 additional sheets of overlapping plastic wrap. Roll dough, still covered, into a 12 x 8-inch rectangle. Place dough in freezer 5 minutes or until plastic wrap can easily be removed. Remove top sheets of plastic wrap.

Place vanilla dough on top of chocolate dough, plastic wrap side up.

Remove plastic wrap from vanilla dough; turn dough over onto a lightly floured surface. Remove plastic wrap from chocolate dough.

Cut dough stack in half crosswise to form 2 (8 x 6-inch) rectangles.

Stack one rectangle on top of the other, alternating vanilla and chocolate doughs; wrap in plastic wrap. Freeze 10 minutes or until firm and plastic wrap can easily be removed.

Cut the dough crosswise into 6 (6 x 1 1/3-inch) strips. Stack 2 strips on top of each other to form a stack, alternating vanilla and chocolate to form a striped pattern; wrap in plastic wrap, pressing gently.

Repeat procedure with remaining 4 strips to form 2 stacks (there will be 3 stacks total). Chill 30 minutes or until very firm.

Preheat oven to 375°.

Working with 1 stack at a time, unwrap dough. Carefully slice each stack into 12 slices. Place dough slices 2 inches apart on baking sheets lined with parchment paper. Bake at 375° for 12 minutes. Cool on pans 5 minutes. Remove cookies from pans; cool completely on wire racks.

Cinnamon Caramel Cookies

Ingredients:

1 white cake mix

1 egg

8 Tablespoons butter, melted

4 ounces cream cheese, softened

2 teaspoons cinnamon

24 Milky Way Simply Caramel Unwrapped Bites

3-4 Tablespoons cinnamon sugar

Preparation:

-Beat together the cake mix, egg, and melted butter until a soft dough forms.

-Add the cream cheese and cinnamon. Beat again until thoroughly combined. Refrigerate for at least 30 minutes.

-Roll the dough into 24 even dough balls. Press each ball flat and place a Milky Way Caramel Bite in the center. Form the cookie dough around the candy bar and roll into a ball again. Roll the cookie dough ball in the cinnamon sugar and place on a baking sheet.

-Bake at 350 degrees for 10 minutes. Remove from the oven and let cool before moving to a piece of parchment paper. Let cool completely. Store in a sealed container on the counter.

-Makes a batch of 24 delicious cookies

M&M Cookies

Ingredients:

1 cup packed brown sugar

1/2 cup white sugar

1 cup shortening

2 eggs

1 1/2 teaspoons vanilla extract

2 1/2 cups all-purpose flour

1 teaspoon baking soda

1 teaspoon salt

1 1/2 cups candy-coated milk chocolate

pieces

Preparation:

1. In a large bowl, mix sugar, eggs, shortening, and vanilla thoroughly. Add flour, salt, and baking soda to creamed mixture. Blend well. Add 3/4 cup of M&M candies.

2. Drop dough by teaspoonful onto cookie sheet. Slightly push a few candies on top of each dough ball with remaining candies.

3. Bake at 350 degrees F (175 degrees C) for 9 to 11 minutes, to your liking.

Red Velvet Cookie Sandwiches

Cookies ingredients:

1 box Red Velvet cake mix

1 egg

¼ cup water

¼ cup vegetable oil

powder sugar

Cream filling ingredients:

1 8oz block of cream cheese, softened

3 tbs butter, softened

1 tsp vanilla

1.5-2 cups powdered sugar

Preparation:

1. Heat oven to 350 degrees F. In a stand mixer or using your own elbow grease with a wooden spoon, mix together cake mix, oil, water and egg. Dough will be sticky. Roll dough into 1 inch balls and drop into a small bowl of powdered sugar.

2. Roll dough balls in powdered sugar and place on a parchment-paper lined baking sheet. Bake 8-10 minutes, until cookies begin to spread and show "crinkle" texture. Cool on

cookie rack.

3. While cookies are cooling, prepare the frosting. Mix the first three ingredients in a stand or hand mixer and slowly add powdered sugar, until desired consistency is reached.

4. When cookies are completely cool, spoon frosting onto one side and sandwich with another cookie. Let set and then enjoy! Store in an airtight container.

Cookies with Green Peas

Ingredients:

520 grams flour

200 grams green peas (ground)

200 grams icing sugar

5 grams fine salt

250ml corn oil

Preparation:

Preheat oven at 150 degree celsius

In a big mixing bowl, combine all ingredients.

Mix all to become soft dough.

You can either roll out to a sheet of 3/4" and use cookies cutter or use a cookies mould.

Place cookies on a pan line with baking sheet and bake for 15 minutes.

Remove and cool it on rack before store in airtight container.

Hot Chocolate-Marshmallow Cookies

ingredients

(Good for 12 servings)

Ingredients

1 roll refrigerated chocolate chip cookie dough

1 cup Chocolate Flavored Hazelnut Spread

3 tablespoons unsweetened baking cocoa

3/4 teaspoon Chili Powder

1/2 teaspoon Cinnamon

6 large marshmallows, cut in half

Preparation:

Heat oven to 350°F. Let cookie dough stand at room temperature 10 minutes to soften. Line 2 large cookie sheets with Reynolds® Parchment Paper.

In large bowl, break up cookie dough. Add hazelnut spread, cocoa, chili powder and cinnamon. Beat with electric mixer on low speed about 2 minutes or until well blended.

Shape dough into 12 (2-inch) balls. Flatten each ball into 3-inch round. Shape 1 cookie dough round around 1 marshmallow half, covering completely. Repeat with remaining dough rounds and marshmallows. Place 2 inches apart on cookie sheets.

Bake 10 to 13 minutes or until surface of cookie appears cracked and marshmallow shows through. Cool 5 minutes; remove from cookie sheets to cooling racks. Cool 5 minutes. Serve warm. Store tightly covered.

Coconut Balls (No baked style)

Ingredients:

1/3 cup Butter

3 Tbsp. Water

1 Tsp. Vanilla Extract

2 cups sifted Powdered Sugar

1/2 cup Milk Powder

3 cups sweetened Flaked Coconut

1 cup (6 ounces) semisweet chocolate, chopped

Procedure:

1. Melt 1/3 cup butter in a medium saucepan over low heat. Remove from heat, and stir in 3 tablespoons water and vanilla.

2. Combine powdered sugar and milk powder; stir 1/2 cup at a time into butter mixture until smooth. Stir in coconut.

3. Shape into 1-inch balls, and place on ungreased baking sheets. Chill 20 minutes.

4. Place chocolate in a small zip-top freezer bag; seal. Submerge

in hot water until chocolate melts. Snip a tiny hole in one corner of bag, and drizzle chocolate over coconut balls. Store in Refrigerator.

Coconut Chocolate No-bake Macaroons

Ingredients:

3 cups unsweetened dried coconut flakes

3/4 cup almond flour*

3/4 cup cocoa powder

1 cup maple syrup

1/3 cup coconut oil, melted

1 tablespoon vanilla extract

1/2 teaspoon salt

Procedure:

Mix all ingredients together well. Form into small balls using a spoon or cookie scoop and refrigerate until firm.

Servings: Yields about 40 macaroons

Note:

*You can grind your own almond flour by placing whole almonds in a blender/food processor and blending until a fine meal.

Caramel Golden No Bake Cookies

Ingredients:

2 cups brown sugar

1/2 cup milk

1/4 cup butter

1/2 cup creamy peanut butter

3 1/2 cups quick oats

1 cup coconut (optional)

1 teaspoon vanilla

Preparation:

In saucepan, mix sugar, milk, and butter.

Boil for one minute, stirring constantly.

Remove from heat and stir in the remaining ingredients.

Drop by tablespoons onto waxed paper and let sit for 5-10 minutes or

until firm.

Brownies with almonds

Ingredients:

1/2 cup unsweetened chocolate chips

2/3 cup all purpose flour

1/3 cup unsalted butter

1/2 tsp baking powder

3/4 cup white sugar

1 tsp coffee powder

1 tsp vanilla extract

1/8 tsp salt

1 pc egg

chopped almonds

Preparation:

1. In a bowl, melt the chocolate chips.

2. In a separate bowl, beat the egg, then add the sugar gradually. Mix well.

3. Add the softened butter, melted chocolate, salt and baking powder. Mix thoroughly until smooth.

4. Add the flour gradually and mix well. (Do not add all at once!)

5. Add the vanilla extract and coffee powder, then mix until all ingredients are well combined.

6. Preheat oven to 150 ºC.

7. Pour the mixture on a baking pan. (Note: If you are not using a non-stick baking pan, you have to grease it first.)

8. Sprinkle the chopped almonds on top.

9. Bake for 30-40 minutes or until toothpick comes out clean.

10. Remove the brownies from the oven and let it cool down.

11. Slice and place it on a serving plate, then serve.